+ MEDICAL ACADEMY

DOCTOR

IN TRAINING

+ MEDICAL ACADEMY

STUDENT PASS

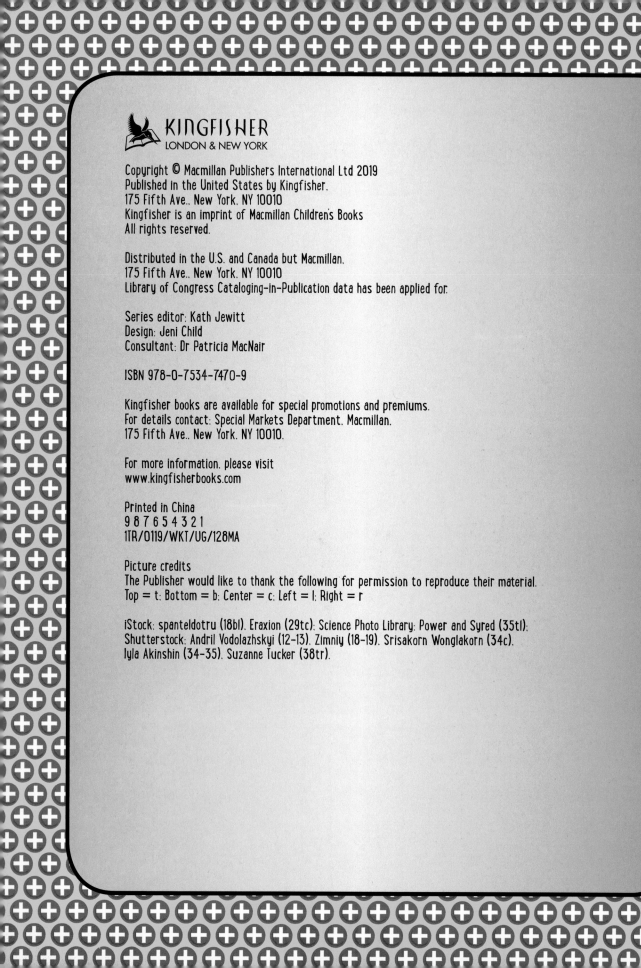

KINGFISHER
LONDON & NEW YORK

Copyright © Macmillan Publishers International Ltd 2019
Published in the United States by Kingfisher.
175 Fifth Ave., New York, NY 10010
Kingfisher is an imprint of Macmillan Children's Books
All rights reserved.

Distributed in the U.S. and Canada but Macmillan.
175 Fifth Ave., New York, NY 10010
Library of Congress Cataloging-in-Publication data has been applied for.

Series editor: Kath Jewitt
Design: Jeni Child
Consultant: Dr Patricia MacNair

ISBN 978-0-7534-7470-9

Kingfisher books are available for special promotions and premiums.
For details contact: Special Markets Department, Macmillan.
175 Fifth Ave., New York, NY 10010.

For more information, please visit
www.kingfisherbooks.com

Printed in China
9 8 7 6 5 4 3 2 1
1TR/0119/WKT/UG/128MA

Picture credits
The Publisher would like to thank the following for permission to reproduce their material.
Top = t; Bottom = b; Center = c; Left = l; Right = r

iStock: spanteldotru (18bl), Eraxion (29tc); Science Photo Library: Power and Syred (35tl);
Shutterstock: Andril Vodolazhskyi (12-13), Zimniy (18-19), Srisakorn Wonglakorn (34c),
Iyla Akinshin (34-35), Suzanne Tucker (38tr).

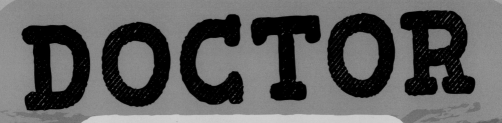

DOCTOR
IN TRAINING

←--- Can you find me
on every page?

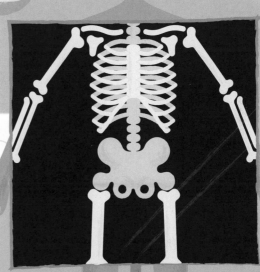

KINGFISHER
LONDON & NEW YORK

MEDICAL ACADEMY

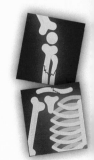

TRAINING PROGRAM

THEORY

THEORY pages are full of important information that you need to know.

PRACTICAL

PRACTICAL pages have a task to do or a doctor skill to acquire.

THEORY 1

TRAINING TIME

So, you want to be a doctor?
Are you a good listener?
Can you stay calm in a crisis?
Not bothered by icky stuff?
Then congratulations! Your
medical training starts today.

WHAT'S THE JOB?

Doctors help people stay healthy.
They know lots about the human body,
and how to make sick people better.

Every day a doctor has to . . .

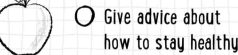

O Give advice about
how to stay healthy.

O See patients in the clinic
or hospital, visit them
at home, or talk to
them on the phone.

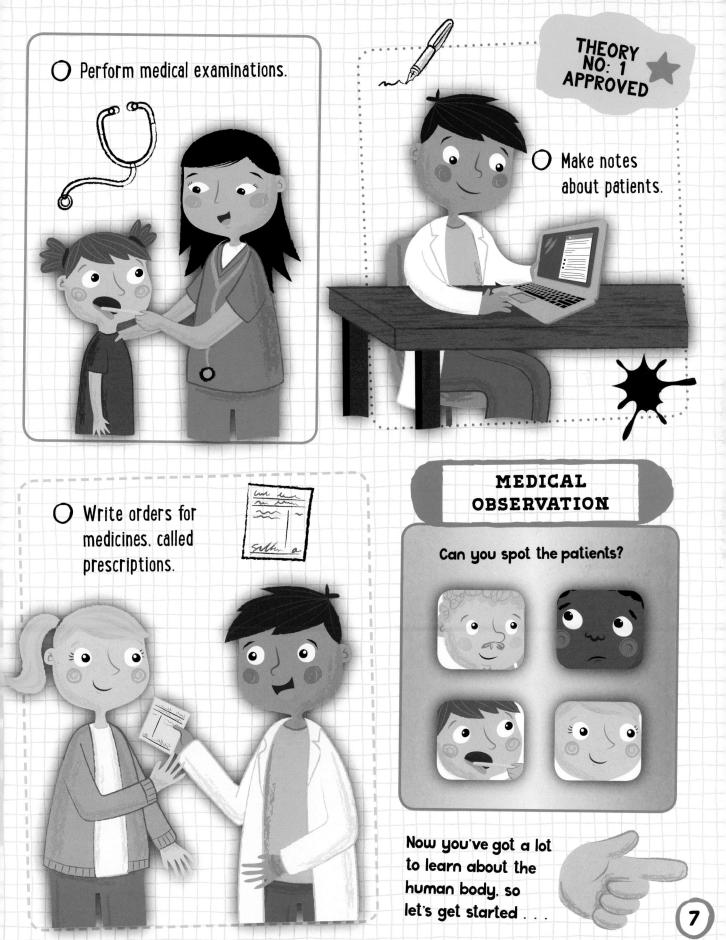

○ Perform medical examinations.

○ Make notes about patients.

○ Write orders for medicines, called prescriptions.

MEDICAL OBSERVATION

Can you spot the patients?

Now you've got a lot to learn about the human body, so let's get started . . .

7

DOCTOR'S KIT

Doctors use special equipment to help them find out what is wrong with a patient. Before you begin your training, you need to collect your tools.

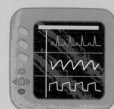

CHECKLIST

Can you find your equipment in the clinic? Try and find each one.

 ○ **Stethoscope** to listen to the heart and lungs

 ○ **Otoscope** to look in the patient's ear

 ○ **Blood pressure monitor** to check how strong the heart is

 ○ **Sample bottle** for collecting urine for testing

 ○ **Penlight** to shine into dark places such as the throat

 ○ **Doctor's bag** to carry all your equipment in

BRILLIANT BODY

Your body is an amazing machine that keeps working all your life. As a doctor you'll need to know about the human body, inside and out, so prepare to discover some brilliant body facts.

BONKERS BONES

The smallest bone in the body is inside the ear. It's about the size of a grain of rice.

BITE SIZE

Children have 20 teeth and adults have 32. Baby teeth fall out and grow back as adult teeth. Enamel—the white coating on your teeth—is the hardest thing in your body.

MASSES OF MUSCLES

There are over 600 muscles in the body, and 43 of them are in the face. The speediest muscle is the one that makes you blink.

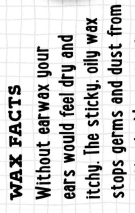

WAX FACTS

Without earwax your ears would feel dry and itchy. The sticky, oily wax stops germs and dust from getting inside your ears.

BELLY BUTTON BUGS

Millions of minuscule living things, called bacteria, make their home inside your belly button.

The skin is the largest organ of your body.

RED AND RUNNY

A 10-year-old has about 4 pints (2 liters) of blood inside the body. That's enough to fill a really big bottle of lemonade.

HEARTY PARTY

3,000,000,000 (or 3 billion) is the number of times your heart might beat in your lifetime.

THEORY NO. 2 APPROVED

HAIRY SCARY

Your body is covered with millions of hairs. The only bald places are the palms of your hands, the bottoms of your feet, and your lips.

HARD AS NAILS

Your nails are made from the same tough stuff as the horns of animals, such as cows and goats.

ACTIVITY

Doctors need to know your kneecaps from your elbows! Can you identify all these body parts in the big picture?

○ knee   ○ ankle   ○ wrist   ○ elbow
○ forehead ○ jaw   ○ shoulder   ○ heel

BLOOD

Blood vessels carry blood to the brain.

Blood is a 24-hour delivery service, carrying important stuff your body needs. It travels along wiggly tubes, called blood vessels, to reach every part of your body.

Your heart is about the size of your fist.

The red tubes are called arteries.

The blue tubes are called veins.

DOCTOR'S NOTES

Delivery
The blood in the red tubes (arteries) travels from the heart around the body, ready to deliver:

food
oxygen
water
medicine
heat

Collection
The blood in the blue tubes (veins) travels back to the heart. It collects:

waste

PRACTICAL NO: 2 APPROVED

CHECKLIST

Can you find these things?

- ◯ **Heart**—this strong muscle pumps the blood throughout the body.

- ◯ **Lungs**—blood picks up an important gas here, called oxygen.

- ◯ **Arteries**—these tubes carry blood away from the heart.

- ◯ **Veins**—these tubes carry blood back to the heart.

- ◯ **Capillaries**—the good stuff in blood passes through these tiny tubes to every part of the body.

- ◯ **Liver**—blood picks up food from here.

- ◯ **Kidneys**—blood delivers the waste stuff from the body here, where it gets cleaned up.

Can you spot the one that doesn't belong in this picture?

Take a look at what is packed into a single drop of blood.

Red blood cells carry oxygen to every part of the body.

White blood cells attack and destroy germs.

Platelets make your blood sticky to stop the bleeding when you cut yourself.

Plasma half of your blood is watery stuff that carries food and medicine to parts of the body.

ODD ONE OUT

THE HEART

Bom-bom, bom-bom. That's the sound of the hardworking heart beating. It pushes blood through your body every second of every single day. It can change the amount of blood pumped and how fast it beats.

The right side of the heart pumps blood to the lungs to pick up oxygen.

Right atrium

Va

Right ventricle

The heart squeezes to pump blood throughout the body. Each squeeze is one heartbeat.

A stethoscope makes it easier to listen to your heart beating.

The heart is a powerful muscle in the middle of your chest.

The left side of the heart collects blood from the lungs and pumps it out to the body.

Left atrium

alves

The valves inside your heart are like doors. The thump of your heartbeat is the sound of them opening and closing with each pump of the heart.

Left ventricle

FIND THE DIFFERENCES

Heart monitor machines make a record of your heartbeat on a screen. Can you find 6 differences between the two screens?

TAKING YOUR PULSE

Your pulse rate is the number of times your heart beats in one minute. You can feel your pulse in your wrist because the blood flows near to the surface.

1 Hold out one hand, palm up. Press two fingers on your wrist below the thumb until you feel thumping.

2 Use a watch to count the number of thumps in one minute.

PRACTICAL NO: 3 APPROVED

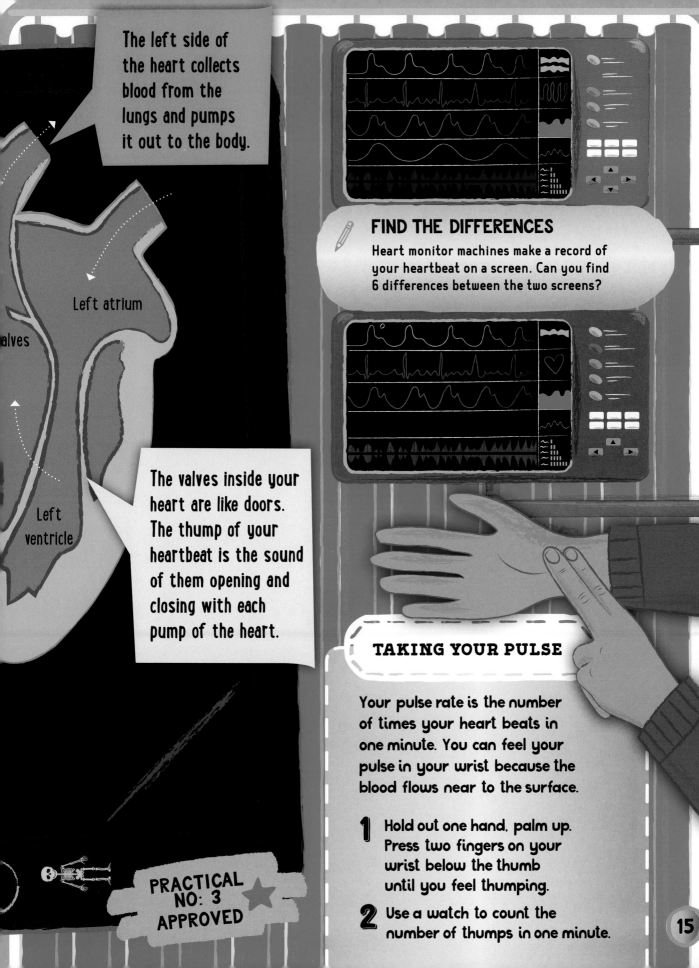

BREATHING

Use your stethoscope to listen to your patient's chest as they breathe in. The lungs fill with air and give the body a boost of oxygen—the gas we need to stay alive.

BREATHE IN

1 Air travels through your mouth or nose. Hairs and mucus trap dust and dirt and stop it from getting into your lungs.

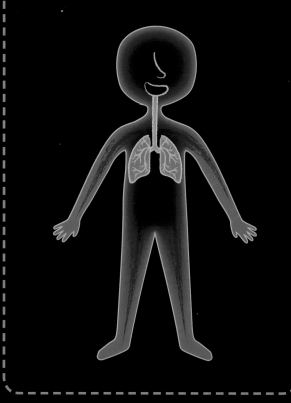

2 The air warms up as it travels down the windpipe and into the lungs.

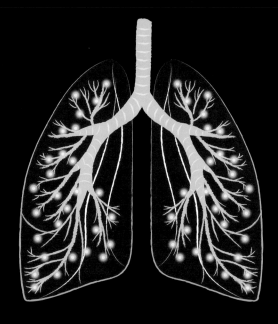

3 Inside the lungs, air travels down lots of tubes that get smaller and branch out, just like a tree.

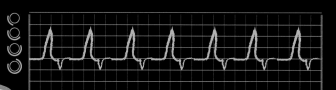
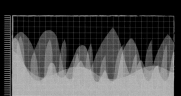
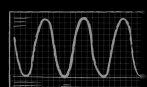

ACTIVITY

When you exercise, your body needs more oxygen so you breathe faster. Do 10 jumping jacks on the spot, then stop. Are you breathing faster now?

You breathe in and out about 20,000 times a day without even thinking about it!

4 At the end of every little tube is an air sac covered in tiny blood vessels.

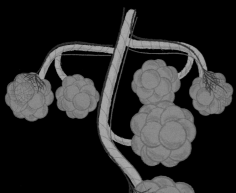

5 This is where the oxygen in the air passes into the blood and is carried off around the body.

BREATHE OUT

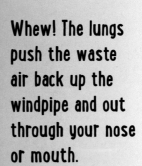

Whew! The lungs push the waste air back up the windpipe and out through your nose or mouth.

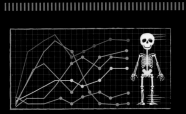

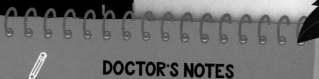

DOCTOR'S NOTES

Coughs and sneezes

If anything blocks the air on its way to the lungs, the body gets rid of it with a cough or a sneeze.

When we cough or sneeze, air shoots out of the nose and mouth, along with mucus and germs. ACHOO! So make sure to wash your hands regularly if you have a cough or cold.

Your skeleton is made of hundreds of bones, connected to give the body its shape and protect the soft parts inside. Without bones you would be a floppy blob.

BONES

SKULL
Your skull is like a helmet, protecting the soft brain inside it.

Adult skeletons have 206 bones, while babies' skeletons have 270.

SPINE
The spine has 33 bones that fit together like building blocks. Run your finger along your back. Can you feel the lumpy bones?

RIBS
Ribs protect your heart and lungs.

ELBOW
This is the elbow joint. Joints are places where two bones meet. They allow your skeleton to move.

THIGH
Your thighbone is the largest bone in the body.

Bone is living tissue. It is hard and strong, but lots of little holes inside make it light, so you can move easily.

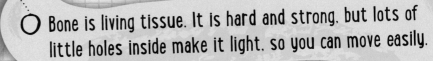

KEEPING BONES HEALTHY

STRONG BONES

Eating food with plenty of calcium keeps bones healthy and strong. Calcium is found in milk and foods made from milk.

BROKEN BONES

Sometimes bones break or crack. As a doctor, you will need to check for breaks if a patient has an injury that is sore and swollen. An X-ray is a picture that shows the bones underneath the skin and muscle.

TREATMENT

Doctors sometimes wrap the broken bone in a hard bandage, called a cast, to keep it very still. Then new bone can grow to mend the break.

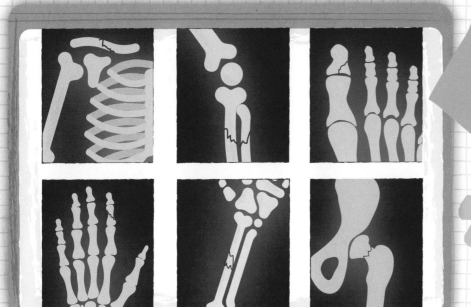

Can you find the broken bone in each of these X-ray pictures?

PRACTICAL NO: 5 APPROVED

1 MUSCLES TO MOVE

Long, stretchy muscles are attached to your skeleton. They pull on the bones to make them move. You are in charge, so they only work when you want them to.

2 MUSCLE MAGIC

Some muscles work without you having to think about them. Right now, deep inside your body, muscles are busy mixing food in your tummy, squashing food in your gut, and squeezing the blood in your arteries to push it along.

THEORY 3

MUSCLES

THEORY NO: 3 APPROVED

Muscles make parts of your body move. Whether you are walking or sleeping, somewhere in the body, muscles are hard at work.

3 MUSCLE MARATHON

The most hardworking muscle in your body is the heart. It squeezes to pump the blood around your body at least 70 times every minute your whole life.

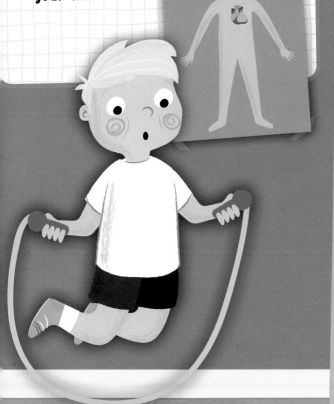

MIGHTY MUSCLES

Exercise makes your muscles bigger and stronger. Eating foods that have protein in them helps build strong muscles too.

BEND . . . AND STRAIGHTEN

Bend your arm while you squeeze the top with your other hand. Can you feel the muscle bulging?

1 When you bend your arm, the muscle gets shorter.

2 When you straighten your arm, the muscle gets longer.

DOCTOR'S NOTES

What is a pulled muscle?

If you make a muscle work too hard or too fast, you might tear part of the muscle. This painful damage is called "pulling a muscle."

There are lots of fun ways to exercise your muscles. Activities such as cycling are great for strengthening your muscles.

DIGESTION

What is going on in your patient's tummy? As part of your training, you will need to know the ins and outs of the grumbly, gurgling guts.

FOOD FOR FUEL

Your body gets energy from the food that you eat. For food to turn into fuel for the body, it needs to be broken into tiny pieces. This is called digestion.

It can take up to 3 days for food to travel all the way through your body.

Saliva glands

PRACTICAL NO: 6 APPROVED

22

RUMBLE! RUMBLE!

Your tummy grumbles if your stomach churns when it is empty. The gases inside of it make a growling sound.

CHECKLIST

Find each body part on the big picture.

- ○ Food is chewed in the mouth by teeth and mixed with spit, called saliva, to make it mushy.

- ○ Each mouthful travels down a tube called the esophagus (say uh-sof-a-gus). Muscles in the tube push the food into the stomach.

- ○ The muscly walls of the stomach mix and churn the food. Strong stomach juices turn the lumps into liquid.

- ○ This tube is the small intestine. The good parts in the food pass through its walls and are delivered around the body.

- ○ The stuff left behind is waste. It travels to the large intestine. Here, water is sucked out of the leftovers, and it is turned into poop.

START

EXIT

Find your way through the small intestine maze to the large intestine.

DISTANCE TRAVELED: 26 feet (8 meters)

DOCTOR'S NOTES

Tummy troubles

If you eat harmful food or catch a tummy bug, the stomach gets rid of it by sending the food back out of your mouth as vomit.

Sometimes germs or bugs get into your intestines. The body gets rid of them by making you poop more often. This is called diarrhea (say die-o-ree-al).

WATERWORKS

Gulp a glass of water, and before long you need to pee. But what is this watery stuff that we flush away, and how is it made? As a doctor in training, it's your job to find out!

○ Kidney

○ Blood vessels

○ Bladder

URINE

Urine is made up of water and other waste stuff that the body doesn't need.

1 Water from eating and drinking passes into your blood. Your blood flows through your kidneys on its journey around the body.

2 The kidneys are the body's cleaning machines. They get rid of waste and extra water as urine.

3 Drip, drip— urine trickles down tubes into the bladder all day long.

4 When the bladder is full, you need to use the toilet and the urine gushes out.

Follow each pipe to see which one has the leak.

a b c

WATER

Two-thirds of your body is water, but you lose water all the time when you sweat, breathe, and go to the toilet.

Your body needs at least 6 glasses of water every day to keep it filled up.

DOCTOR'S NOTES

If you drink plenty, the body makes lots of urine. If you don't drink much, the body saves water and makes a small amount of strong urine. A doctor can tell if a patient is drinking enough by the color of their urine.

THEORY NO: 4 APPROVED

DIP TEST

Match the patient's urine with the correct color on the chart. Did the patient drink enough water today?

Need to drink lots of water	Drink some water	Need to drink a little water	Good! Drinking plenty

BEING HEALTHY

You need to take care of your body to keep it in shape. It will be part of your job to advise people how to stay healthy.

FAB FOOD

You need to eat lots of different foods to give your body everything it needs.

Carbohydrates give you energy to play and do sports.

Fruit and vegetables are packed with vitamins that keep your body healthy.

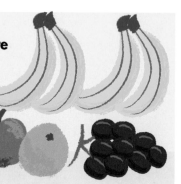

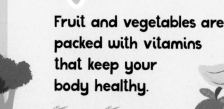

Find one healthy food from each group to go in your lunchbox.

Pick a healthy drink too.

DOCTOR'S NOTES

You might be asleep, but some parts of your body never rest.

- The brain dreams and keeps alert to loud noises.
- Skin mends cuts and bruises.
- The heart keeps beating.
- The lungs keep breathing air.
- The stomach and intestines digest food.
- The kidneys keep making urine.
- Bones keep growing.

THEORY NO: 5 APPROVED

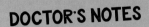

Fat gives you a store of energy, but you only need a small amount of it.

Protein helps your body grow and mend itself.

SUPER SLEEP
Sleeping gives your body a chance to rest and repair itself.

Babies need lots of sleep. 15 to 20 hours altogether!

GROWING
The body needs more sleep when it is young and still growing.

ZZZZZZ

Young children need 10 to 12 hours' sleep each day.

DREAMS
You dream every night, but you might not always remember your dreams. Can you remember what you dreamed about last night?

Teenagers need 8 to 10 hours' sleep.

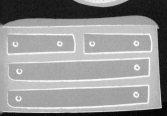

Grown-ups need about 8 hours' sleep each night.

sneezing and
coughing

swollen,
itchy
eyes

SYMPTOMS

Allergies make people feel
sick in different ways.

- runny nose
- sneezing
- swollen, itchy eyes
- coughing
- wheezing chest
- vomiting
- upset tummy
- itchy rashes

itchy rashes

PRACTICAL 7

ALLERGIES

An allergy is when something that is
normally harmless makes you feel ill.
For the next part of your training,
head for the park to spot all the
things that can cause allergies.

UNDER THE MICROSCOPE

Dust mites are very tiny creatures that live in every home. You can't see them or feel them, but some people are allergic to their teeny poos.

wheezing chest

upset tummy

vomiting

runny nose

How many bees are in the picture?

CHECKLIST

Can you find all of the different things that cause allergies?

- ○ **Nuts**, such as hazelnuts, almonds, and peanuts
- ○ **Pollen** is the dust made by flowers that floats in the air
- ○ **Insect stings**, especially wasp and bee stings
- ○ **Fish** and **shellfish**, such as shrimp
- ○ **Wheat**, found in bread, cookies, and cake
- ○ **Milk** and foods made from milk
- ○ **Fur** from animals

29

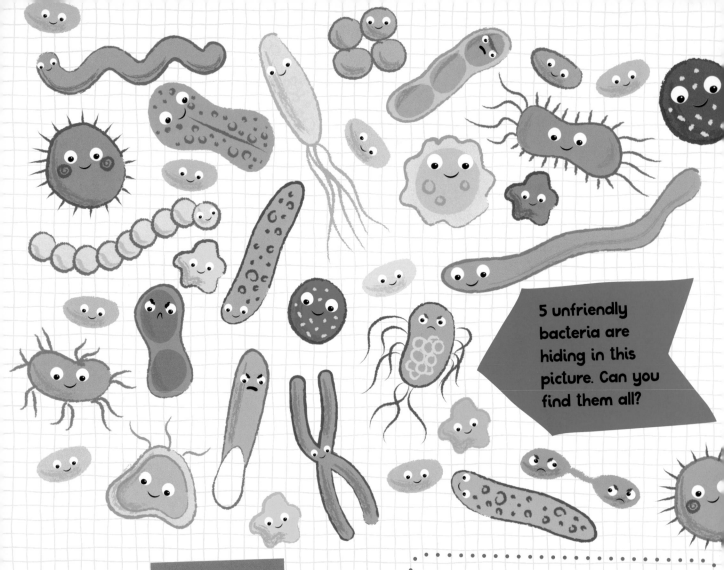

5 unfriendly bacteria are hiding in this picture. Can you find them all?

BATTLING BUGS

We are surrounded by millions of tiny living things called bacteria. These are found just about everywhere on our planet. Some are good and some are bad, so it's a doctor's job to help people keep the bad ones away.

GOODIES AND BADDIES

Lots of bacteria are harmless, and many are good for us. Your stomach and intestines are full of friendly bacteria that help you digest your food and fight off illness.

Some kinds of bacteria can make you sick if they get inside your body. We call them germs.

WHERE DO GERMS LIVE?

○ On old or moldy food and raw meat.

○ On the soles of your shoes and on the ground where they walk.

○ On your hands and things that have been touched by lots of other people's hands.

○ Coughs and sneezes are full of germs.

KEEP THEM OUT!

Your body has lots of **smart ways** of keeping out germs.

1 **Nose**: germs in the air that you breathe get caught by tiny hairs and slimy mucus.

2 **Eye**: tears wash away germs.

3 **Ears**: earwax slowly flows out of your ears, taking germs and dirt with it.

4 **Skin**: this protective cover all over your body helps stop germs from getting inside.

✎ DOCTOR'S NOTES

How to protect against germs:

Wash your hands after going to the toilet, touching anything dirty, and before you eat.

Cover your mouth and nose when you cough or sneeze, then wash your hands.

1

2

3

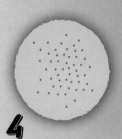

4

THEORY NO: 6 APPROVED

MEDICINES

Our body is good at taking care of itself, but sometimes we need help to get better, or to keep us safe from diseases. As a trainee doctor, it's time for you to get the lowdown on medicines.

DOCTOR'S WARNING

BE SAFE WITH MEDICINES!

1. Never take a medicine that is not for you—it could make you really sick.

2. Never take more than it says you need.

3. Grown-ups are in charge of giving medicines.

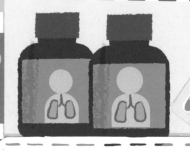

If patients are sick they might need medicine to help them feel better.

VACCINATIONS

A tiny amount of the germ that causes the illness is injected into the body. It's not enough to make you ill, but the body learns to fight the germ, protecting you from it in the future.

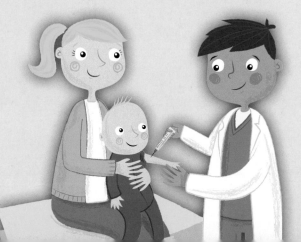

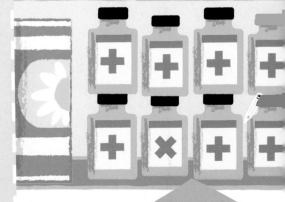

Can you spot the one that doesn't match in the bottles above?

Some medicines fight illnesses by killing the germs inside the body. These are called antibiotics.

Some medicines soothe pain, such as from an earache or a sore throat. They can't make you well, but they make you feel better while you are recovering.

People with asthma find it hard to breathe. They use an inhaler with medicine inside to open up the breathing tubes and help them breathe more easily.

Some medicines cannot be swallowed, so they have to be injected instead.

PRESCRIPTIONS

Can you find these medicines on the shelves?

O Cough medicine

O Skin rash cream

O Eye drops

PRACTICAL
NO: 8
APPROVED

SKIN

Your skin is a stretchy covering that wraps around your whole body. It may seem smooth and unexciting, but take a closer look—there's important stuff happening just under the surface!

WATERPROOFING

The top layer of skin is waterproof. That's why you don't fill up with water when you take a bath or go swimming.

SUN PROTECTION

The skin stops your insides from drying out in the sun's heat. It also contains melanin, which stops your skin from burning.

○ People with lots of melanin have darker skin.

○ Freckles and moles are small patches of skin with lots of melanin.

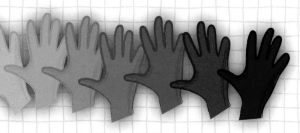

! DOCTOR'S WARNING!

Sun safety
Too much sunshine can damage skin. All patients should:

1. Put on plenty of sunscreen.
2. Cover up with a hat and a T-shirt.
3. Stay in the shade during the hottest time of the day.

GERM CONTROL

Skin helps stop dirt and germs from getting inside your body so take care of your skin!

SKIN SPOT

Look closely at your skin. Can you find any of the below?

○ freckle   ○ hair
○ mole   ○ sweat pore

FLAKY STUFF

Thousands and thousands of flakes of dead skin fall off your body every minute.

HAIRY

The hairs on your skin stand up when you are cold. This traps a layer of air to keep you warm.

HEATING

A layer of fat under your skin acts like a blanket to keep you warm.

This is a picture of what is under your skin.

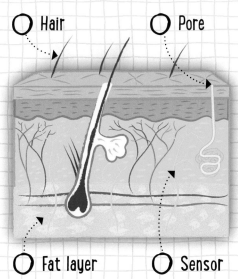

○ Hair   ○ Pore

○ Fat layer   ○ Sensor

COOLING

Sweat comes out of tiny holes called pores. When sweat dries on your skin it cools you down.

FEELING

Sensors in your skin tell you when you touch something hot or cold, wet or dry, smooth or sharp.

THEORY 8

CUTS AND BRUISES

Bumps, cuts, and scrapes are all part of life for your skin. Luckily, it is very good at repairing itself. Before you can even reach for your doctor's bag, the body is already on the case.

ACTIVITY

Can you spot...
- ◯ a blister
- ◯ a cut finger
- ◯ a bruise

on these pages?

When you cut your skin, blood spills out. Special blood cells, called platelets, leap into action to plug the hole. They make your blood thick and sticky. This is called clotting.

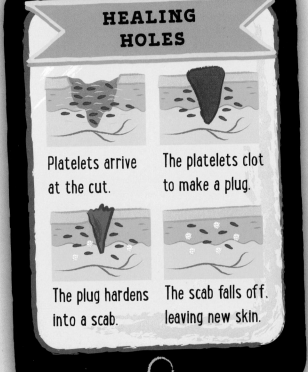

HEALING HOLES

Platelets arrive at the cut.

The platelets clot to make a plug.

The plug hardens into a scab.

The scab falls off, leaving new skin.

When you bump yourself, tiny blood vessels break and blood leaks out underneath your skin. This is called a bruise. The bruise goes through some colorful changes as it heals.

LUMPS AND BUMPS

DAY 1

DAY 3

DAY 5

DAY 7

A blister is a round bubble of clear liquid under the skin. Blisters form when the skin is rubbed, so you might get one on your heel if your shoe rubs, or on your hand from holding a racket to hit a ball.

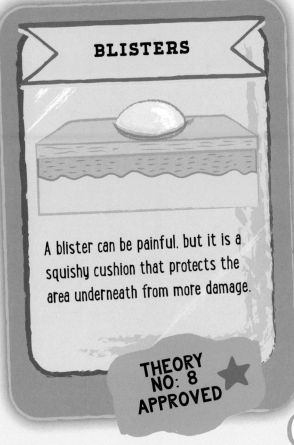

BLISTERS

A blister can be painful, but it is a squishy cushion that protects the area underneath from more damage.

THEORY
NO: 8
APPROVED

DOCTOR'S NOTES

DO put a bandage on a cut or blister to keep it clean until it starts to heal.

DON'T pick scabs or pop blisters! You could let germs get under the skin.

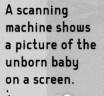

A scanning machine shows a picture of the unborn baby on a screen.

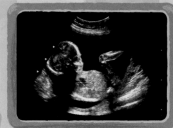

Being a doctor means taking care of everybody, from tiny babies and young children to grown-ups and old people. Doctors even take care of babies before they are born!

PRACTICAL 9

GROWING

From the moment a baby is born, its body is growing and its brain is learning. Match each picture with the right description.

○ Bella spends time with friends. She can do a lot of things on her own—and she's growing very fast.

80 YEARS OLD

○ Bella cries, feeds, and sleeps for most of the day.

5 YEARS OLD

25 YEARS OLD

BABIES

It's hard to believe that a baby starts life as a tiny speck, smaller than a pinhead.

The father's sperm joins with the mother's egg and the baby begins to grow in the mother's womb.

Egg

Sperm

GETTING BIGGER

The baby changes every week as it grows inside the mother. It takes 9 months, or about 40 weeks, before the baby is ready to be born.

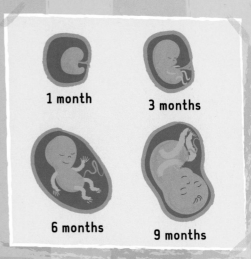

1 month

3 months

6 months

9 months

Bella has wrinkled skin and gray hair. She needs to wear glasses.

10 YEARS OLD

Bella has lost some of her baby teeth now, and big ones are starting to grow. She is learning to read, write, and do sums.

Measure how tall you are. Then keep a record and see how much you grow during 1 year.

NEWBORN

Bella has reached her full size. She can have babies of her own.

Everyone looks different, but families share a lot of the same features, such as hair color. This is because parents pass on their genes to their children.

PRACTICAL 10

FAMILIES

PRACTICAL NO: 10 APPROVED

The waiting room is packed with families waiting to see the doctor! Can you help the receptionist match up the children with their parents?

40

The genes you get from your parents control lots of things about the way you are. Look at the things in this list. Do you share any of these features with members of your family?

- ○ eye color
- ○ hair color
- ○ left or right-handed
- ○ straight hair
- ○ curly hair
- ○ freckles
- ○ nose shape

Genes are like a set of instructions that make you the way you are. Children get some of their genes from their father and some from their mother.

Brothers and sisters often look similar because they share a lot of the same genes.

Identical twins look the same because nearly all their genes are the same.

41

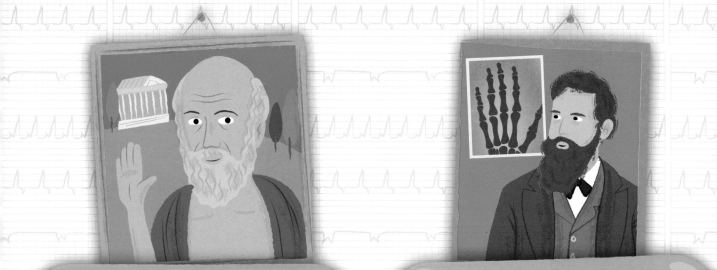

HIPPOCRATES

Hippocrates was a doctor in ancient Greece. His ideas about medicine and disease were so exciting and new that he is still known as the "father of medicine."

WILHELM RONTGEN

Wilhelm discovered how to take pictures that showed the bones inside the body. This made it much easier to repair breaks. He called the pictures X-rays.

ELIZABETH GARRETT ANDERSON

Elizabeth Garrett Anderson was the first woman to qualify as a doctor in the UK. She worked hard to provide medical care for women and children, and she set up the first hospital to be staffed by women.

EDWARD JENNER

Edward Jenner was the first doctor to vaccinate people against a disease called smallpox. The vaccination saved thousands of lives and smallpox was beaten. Thanks to him there are now vaccinations for lots of diseases.

HALL OF FAME

ELIZABETH BLACKWELL

Elizabeth was the first modern-day woman to go to college and become a doctor of medicine in the US. She opened The Medical College for Women, so other women could train to be doctors and surgeons too.

ALEXANDER FLEMING

Fleming discovered the first antibiotic when he noticed that mold growing on one of his germ specimens had killed the bacteria. Antibiotics have saved millions of lives since then.

WILLIAM T.G. MORTON

People used to have operations without anything to take away the pain. William T.G. Morton was the first person to use an anesthetic, making operations painless for the first time.

JANE WRIGHT

Jane Wright was a brilliant doctor and surgeon who worked in medical research, developing new and better ways to treat different kinds of cancer.

These people have all played a part in saving lives and beating disease with their important work.

EXAMINATION

Now it's time to see how much you have learned.

1 What is the name of the paper that has a patient's medicine written on it?
   a) description
   b) prescription
   c) preschool

2 What tool does a doctor use to listen to a patient's heart?
   a) kaleidoscope
   b) telescope
   c) stethoscope

3 Which of these things would you not find on your skin?
   a) freckles
   b) moles
   c) voles

4 What is the name of the special gas that your body needs?
   a) oxygen
   b) oxen
   c) smidgen

5 What is the name for the number of beats that the heart makes in a minute?
   a) the drum
   b) the pump
   c) the pulse rate

6 What do you need to mend a broken bone?
   a) a mast
   b) a cast
   c) a fast

7 What are all the bones in your body called?
   a) structure
   b) plankton
   c) skeleton

8 Which of these is a muscle?
   a) the heart
   b) the brain
   c) the nose

9 What is digestion?

    a) a very blocked nose

    b) blockages caused by food in the body

    c) how your body turns food into energy

10 Which of these body parts does NOT break down food?

    a) the stomach

    b) the lungs

    c) the small intestine

11 How many glasses of water do you need to drink each day?

    a) 6

    b) 16

    c) 1

12 What is the proper word for "pee"?

    a) latrine

    b) urine

    c) marine

13 Which sorts of foods should we eat more of?

    a) sweet and sticky

    b) fresh and fruity

    c) fried and salty

14 What is a vaccination?

    a) an examination by the doctor

    b) a test to see if you have caught an illness

    c) something that stops you from catching an illness

MEDICAL SCORES

Check your answers at the back of the book and add up your score.

1 to 5 Oops! Get back to the clinic and study up on your body facts.

6 to 10 You are well on your way to becoming a top doctor.

11 to 14 Top of the class! You really know your stuff, doc!

DICTIONARY

DOCTOR SPEAK

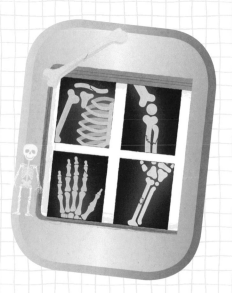

antibiotic
A medicine that kills harmful germs in the body.

bacteria
Tiny living things, some of which cause diseases.

blood vessels
The tubes that carry blood around the body.

calcium
White, chalky stuff that is found in teeth and bones. It is also found in milk and foods made from milk.

carbohydrates
Stuff found in foods, such as bread and pasta, that gives you energy.

digestion
Breaking down the food you eat into energy for your body.

oxygen
The gas in the air that plants and animals need to live.

platelet
A kind of blood cell in the body that stops bleeding.

prescription
A note from a doctor to a pharmacist saying which medicines a patient needs.

protein
Stuff found in food and drink, such as meat, eggs, and milk, that you need to grow and be healthy.

stethoscope
A tool that a doctor uses to listen to your heart and breathing.

vomit
Food and drink that comes back up from the stomach and out of the mouth.

womb
The place inside a woman's body where a baby grows before it is born.

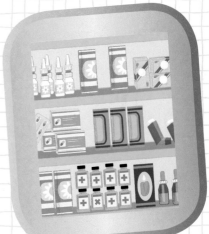

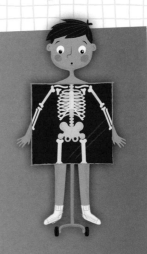

MEDICAL ACADEMY

WELL DONE!

You made it through your doctor training.

FULLY QUALIFIED

Name..

DOCTOR

ANSWERS

Page 6
The things to find are circled below.

Page 8
The things to find are circled below.

Page 10
The things to find are circled to the side.

Page 13
The one that doesn't match is circled below.

The things to find are circled below.

Page 15
The six differences are circled to the side.

Page 19
The broken bones are circled below.

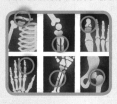

Page 23
The things to find are circled to the side.

Page 23 (bottom)
The path through the maze is shown below.

Page 25
Pipe c has the leak.

Page 29
The things that cause allergies are circled below.

There are 4 bees.

Pages 30-31
The things to find are circled below.

Pages 32-33
The medicines are circled below.

The odd one out is circled.

Pages 36-37
The things to find are circled below.

Pages 38-39
The correct matches are below.

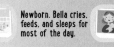

Newborn. Bella cries, feeds, and sleeps for most of the day.

25 years old. Bella has reached her full size.

5 years old. Bella has lost some of her baby teeth.

80 years old. Bella has wrinkled skin and gray hair.

10 years old. Bella spends time with friends.

Pages 38-39
Parents and their children are the same colored circle below.

Pages 44-45
1=b; 2=c; 3=c; 4=a; 5=c; 6=b= 7=c; 8=a; 9=c; 10=b; 11=a; 12=b; 13=b; 14=c.

DO YOU HAVE WHAT IT TAKES TO BECOME A REAL

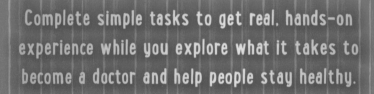

DOCTOR?

Packed with bitesize information,
DOCTOR IN TRAINING will teach you all about
the amazing human body and how to care for it.

Complete simple tasks to get real, hands-on
experience while you explore what it takes to
become a doctor and help people stay healthy.

... IN TRAINING encourages children to get excited
about STEAM subjects and the incredible jobs
linked to them. From doctor to engineer,
kids can learn about the skills and know-how
needed to do one of these amazing jobs.

ILLUSTRATED BY SARAH LAWRENCE
WRITTEN BY CATHERINE ARD

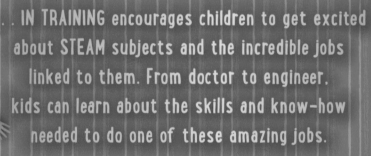

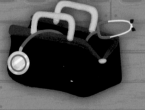

ALSO IN THE SERIES:
ASTRONAUT IN TRAINING
ENGINEER IN TRAINING
SCIENTIST IN TRAINING

COMING SOON:
FIREFIGHTER IN TRAINING
VET IN TRAINING

KINGFISHER
KNOW|WONDER
www.kingfisherbooks.com

USD $8.99 / CAN $11.99
ISBN-13: 978-0-7534-7470-9

50899 >

9 780753 474709